BITTER SWEET MEMORIES

by

Sandra E. Potts

Printed in the United States of America

First Printing, 2014

Edited by Giselle James

Dedication

This book is dedicated to my late mother and father, Lilla Berry-Benjamin (Atla), and Cleveland Berry(Chico), my sisters, Jeanette (Jean), Vinett (Pam), Doreen, and Karen (Paula), and to my brothers, Tony (Jah Stone), Carl (Breda), Orville (Al), and Jeffrey (Jeff), and in memory of my late brother, Sherman.

I also dedicate this collection of stories to my husband, Wendell (Weejay) and my son Christopher. In sharing my life stories, it is my hope that they'll come to understand me better, and recognize, finally, why my love cannot be contained...... My love is bigger than even me!

Acknowledgements

I am deeply indebted to you, my friends and family who never once complained when I called soliciting your opinions at any hour of the day or night. This book would not have been published without your encouragement and support.

Special thanks to my lifelong friend and editor of this book, Professor Giselle James, who has always said, "You have a way with words," and encouraged me to publish my collection of short stories. Thank you for the countless, unselfish hours spent editing and re-editing my writings. I am extremely grateful for your support and guidance; I could not have accomplished this without you!

I would be remiss if I failed to thank my sister and friend, Vinett Steigerwalt, who has supported me and listened to my stories over and over, yet never got tired of hearing them. Thank you for being so wonderfully you!

To Lance and Christine Malcolm, my darling cousins, I am indebted to you both for helping me launch this project.

To my husband, Wendell, and son, Christopher, thanks to you both for giving me the space to fulfill my dream to become a writer! I love you both more than words can express!

To my aunt, Sarah Haynes (Me Auntie), you have been an inspiration and a rock in my life. Thank you for believing in me and for your continuous support.

To my many friends and relatives, (too numerous to mention individually), who have inspired and supported me throughout this journey; I appreciate you all and thank you sincerely!

May God bless all who read this book! My wish is that it will bring inspiration and joy to all your hearts. Thank you!

Contents

Introduction

My love of writing started when I was sent to live with relatives. Every week I would write to my family and I tried to paint pictures with my words so that they could see what I see and be a part of my life. I tried to draw them into my world, a world that was very lonely without them.

The few very precious memories I have of us together as a family, in our home in Portland, Jamaica, have sustained me through many difficult periods in my life. The incredible love I have for each member of my family has pulled me out of many dungeons of despair; to surge forth with more vigor, and a greater sense of purpose; I live for them! Their pain is my pain and their joy is my joy!

This book is intended to share with them bitter-sweet memories of my life to help bridge the gap between us. Three specific memories have wounded me deeply and have shaped the course of my life; the memory of my father not recognizing me when we all stood at his death bed. The memory of my siblings telling me that I was cold as ice when I stood at my father's grave and could not cry, and the memory of being told that perhaps I was the 'mule' in the family, when I could not have a child.

I have since striven to let people I care about feel my love, in my every word, thought and deed. I prayed day in and day out to conceive a child and would have done anything, including the impossible, to have at least one. God was merciful and I thank Him for my son, Christopher; now I spend my life writing my pain.

The Decision

When I was twelve years old, the decision was made to send me to Kingston to live with my Godmother, Vera Duncan. The plan was to give me an opportunity to succeed, to give me a better life they said; a chance to attend fine schools, and become "somebody". Hopefully, I would be the one to pull them out of poverty.

I was not happy with their decision, so when the big gold skylark pulled up at the gate, and uncle Chickadee stepped out, I bolted in fear. My mother caught me in the yard by the pepper tree and the clothesline post. I trembled with fear and cried, "Why me! Why me! Me naw go! Me naw go!" "Hush, hush, silly pickney," my mother said. "Of all my ten children, it has to be you!

You are the one with the heart to look back. You're the gift! I am not giving you away; I am giving you a chance. Hush, hush, Sandra, someday you will understand!" I saw tears in my mother's eyes. Then my father spoke, "If you're not happy, send word and we will come get you. If it's one banana seed we have, we will all eat it. Know you always have a home right here!" I had no doubt, that my parents loved me, and contemplating their words brought me comfort. I dried my tears with the hem of my well worn blue dress, and looked around at my brothers and sisters, all wide-eyed and sad. Then my mother handed me a paper bag with a few pieces of clothing and said, "Take these with you." I peeked in the bag and was shocked; my mother had given the clothes that my sister, Doreen, and I shared.

When Doreen realized that I was given all the Sunday clothes, she started to cry and flung herself in the dirt. "Give them to her", I told my mother. She pushed me into the car and said, "I will not send you with only the clothes on your back, take them!" The tears came again, this time not only for me, but also for my sister Doreen and all my family, as I had no idea, when I would ever see them again.

As the car navigated its way over the many potholes, my brothers and sisters ran barefooted and dirty, alongside, waving and calling my name. "Sandra! Sandra!" Blinded by tears, and the evening dusk, I could only make out their silhouettes and as the car rolled out of sight, I sank down on the cold leather seat and cried myself to sleep.

Mom

I was jolted awake by the scraping of the iron gates on the asphalted driveway. With tear stained face and puffy eyes, I sat up, my heart pounding in my chest. The first thing I noticed was the electric lights mounted on poles, bringing to day the long driveway flanked by beautiful bougainvilleas and throwing shadows among the trees of an extensive, well manicured lawn. The car then pulled up under a huge mango tree in front of a grand house, staircase spiraling to the roof, and a verandah as large as my now far away home. On came the lights, and the large front door opened as we emerged from the car, me carrying my paper bag and Uncle Chickadee holding a small parcel of jerk pork.

Mom, (my godmother), wearing a red house coat with matching bed slippers, stepped onto the verandah and hurried with open arms to embrace me. She tried to make conversation, but when I attempted to speak my voice was caught in my throat. She looked at me and said, "Oh, you must be tired and sleepy, let me get you ready for bed and we can talk in the morning." I was ushered into the house as Uncle Chickadee handed her the parcel, returned to his car and left.

We entered an enormous living room, well-furnished and spotless, and then through a passageway to a beautiful bedroom. Mom handed me a lovely cotton night gown and told me to undress and get ready for bed. She took my worn blue dress, which suddenly looked like a piece of rag against the shiny, spotless tiles, and I never saw it again. Two small beds were in the room with two bedside tables on which sat lamps with shades that matched the sea green walls. She opened one side of a large closet with mirrored doors built into the wall, and told me that all the clothes were mine. She placed the little brown paper bag in the bottom of the closet and left the room. I sat at the edge of the bed, not sure what to do, feeling lost and lonely in this big, beautiful house. She returned shortly with a tray on which were a glass of milk, some crackers and a large piece of cheese. She placed the tray on the bedside table. "Here is a snack, if you'd like to eat something before you go to bed," she said in a sweet, warm voice. I looked at her and immediately I knew she was alright; I knew I would be happy with her. She pulled back the covers and I crawled into the bed and curled up into a ball. Sensing my fear, she said, "You can leave on the lights," as she left the room.

I stayed awake for most of the night, lonely for my sisters and brothers, missing the many pokes from tiny, sometimes dirty feet, as we all shared the one bed in which we slept.....lonely for my father's voice and my mother's Anansie stories.....lonely for my family in our little home in the country.

Life at Shortwood Road

L ife at 67 Shortwood Road was great! Attached to the rear of the house were two extra rooms for a live-in helper and a live-in gardener. I had very few chores and spent my days mostly reading and wandering around the property which was abundant with fruit trees. There were several different types of fruit trees: breadfruit, ackee, pear, coconut, apple, grapefruit, orange, tamarind, cherry, lime, lemon, banana, and eight different types of mangoes. George, the gardener, also planted a small garden with ground provisions, peppers and tomatoes.

To the rear of the property, separated by chain-linked fence, was a farm with animals: cows, goats, sheep, guinea chicks, ducks, fish in a pond, and a large coop where chickens were raised. We also had a great big German shepherd, named Bruno. He was black with specks of brown on his paws and head.

When we had visitors, Mom would tell Bruno to go to the back of the house. Eventually, Bruno learned to run to the back whenever he saw anyone coming up the driveway. Mom then labeled him a dumb dog! But he loved me, and would lie at my feet when I sat under the big Bombay mango tree reading. He followed me to the mailbox daily and he chased the guinea chicks when I visited the farm. Bruno was my friend and companion even after Jackie came to live with us permanently.

Jackie was the daughter of Mr. Baker, a friend of the family. She attended the Stella Maris Catholic School which was directly across the street from our house. He owned a hardware store and operated a bar. At times he found it difficult to pick Jackie up from school on time, so she would stay with Mom until he could pick her up.

Eventually, she stayed and went to school. Mom, Jackie, Icilda, our helper, George, our gardener, and Bruno became my new family.

They say time heals all wounds, and after a few months I stopped feeling that terrible longing in my heart for my family whom I'd left behind, but had not forgotten. Each week I would write to my mother, making sure to paint a vivid picture so she could see what I was experiencing. I told her about everything; my letters were long. When her replies arrived I would sit up in the Julie mango tree and read them a thousand times. I always had questions because my mother's letters were short and not very informative. I would stay awake at nights and imagine I was in the country playing with my brothers and sisters.

My dreams would take me back to playing in the river. I relived moments when I wore the katta, a cloth, or piece of clothing folded and worn as a cushion to take the pressure off the head while carrying water or firewood. I reflected on times when I went to Penn to eat ital food with my Rasta brother, Tony. After eating, we would climb up into a pimento tree and relax while he and our cousin, Banny, beat drums or strum make-shift guitars. I recounted precious memories of us hurrying home from school, not stopping to play, because we were very hungry, and when we got home there was no sign of food; the fire side was cold. We would bawl and roll around in the dirt then pick ourselves up and go in search of apples, mangoes or any fruits to eat. Yes, we knew what it was like to be hungry, but here with Mom, I always had enough to eat. I felt compelled to eat everything on my plate because I found it difficult to let food go to waste. I often wished I could send some to my family.

While I was living in the country I had no idea that we were poor. We were happy and free! Now amongst so much, including two gardeners and two helpers I became aware that we had been living in poverty. It is while at Mom that I began to feel the weight of my family. I promised myself that I would do anything to help each and every one of them to experience what I was experiencing, to do anything to help to lift them out of poverty.

Mr. McFarlane

I was 13 years old and had found my angel! Back, then, I didn't know he was my angel; he was just an 'old' pain in the neck. Approximately 20 years later, I realized he was my angel.

Mr. McFarlane, an 80 year old war veteran would walk past my home every morning, at the same time, on his way to pick up the Daily News. I would watch this tall, neat, frail, old man as he walked slowly, but steadily to and from the store, stopping occasionally to rest or remove pebbles out of his way, with his wooden cane.

One day I went out to ask him why he didn't take the bus. He smiled at me with kind blue eyes and said, "This is my daily exercise." The next day he knocked on our front door, introduced himself to Mom, and asked if I could walk with him to the store. After that day, I became his daily, reluctant, chaperon. He was not the typical old person who wanted to talk about himself; instead he seemed only interested in my well being, and he bombarded me with many questions. At times, I would hurry ahead to encourage him to walk faster. He, however, continued to walk steadily at his own pace, and engaged me in conversations about life; about any old thing. Always, he would share warm words of encouragement and inspiration.

He soon had me holding his arms, walking at his pace, all ears! He had my attention, and unaware that I was being taught the tools to success and survival, I soaked up information on any and every thing, delivered in simple language and parables. When I tried to find an excuse to get a day off from my obligation, he wouldn't accept it. He would say, "tut, tut, excuses are like berries on a tree; you will always find one…you don't look for excuses, they are all around you!" I learned not to make excuses for doing whatever I set my mind to do. I learned to be strong, patient and kind. I learned the meaning of commitment and endurance.

I wonder now, some forty years later, was Mr. McFarlane a well decorated five-star general who led his army with courage and valor, a great leader who lifted the morale of his soldiers. Alas, this I will never know, because then, I didn't care to ask. Forty years later, a tear of shame, that I never even knew his first name. Mr. McFarlane, my angel, who led me to an oasis, a place I now draw from, and share with you!

God Sent an Angel

I was 17 years old and attending one of the top-rated high schools in Jamaica, Wolmer's High School for Girls. Mom had been sick for some time, and life was rapidly changing in our home at Shortwood Road. George still lived on the property and took care of the grounds, but, Mom could only afford to have Icilda come once, or sometimes twice per week. In the beginning, the doctors could not determine what was ailing her but, eventually, she was diagnosed with colon cancer.

Financial resources were depleting quickly, and Jackie and I had to learn to prepare our own meals and take care of the house. Our darling Mom was wasting away before our eyes, and she soon took to her bed; no longer able to get up and help herself. One day she felt unusually ill and said, "I wish Icilda was here, she would know what to do!" Icilda had just left the day before and would not be back for a few days. I looked at this wonderful woman who gave so much to us. I would do anything for her, so I told her I would go and find Icilda. "No!" she said, "Icilda lives in the Grants Pen Ghetto. It's not safe for you to go in there!" Truthfully, I had never been in the ghetto before but I insisted that Jackie and I could go. Jackie opted out and said her father told her she should never go in there. "Mom, I pleaded; I have no money or jewelry for them to steal. I am sure I will be fine". She reluctantly consented, and I headed for the ghetto.

A bridge stood at the entrance of the ghetto. As I walked up the road leading to the bridge, I noticed three young men sitting on the bridge smoking marijuana. I contemplated turning back, but when I thought of mom's condition, I pressed on bravely. I told myself that if I simply walked up to them and said good evening they would realize that I was not afraid of them and they wouldn't harm me. With my heart pounding, I boldly entered the smoke filled bridge and stood in their midst. "Good evening, do you know where Miss Icilda lives?" I asked. After coughing and fanning smoke from his face, one man turned his blood red eyes and looked at me while reaching and running his hand up my legs under my dress. I froze. He sensed my fear and said, "What a nice clean piece of beef God send me, me always wah fe taste one nice ting like you." Soon each man was reaching for his share of me; one squeezing on my breast, another pulling on my underwear. I stood, helpless whimpering, "No! No! Please leave me alone!" Caught like a deer in the headlights, I froze, wanting to scream, to run, but I could do neither.

Finally, I found the strength to kick one of them. He stood up and put a long, sharp knife to my face and said,

"You want me give you a telephone cut, you think you beta than me eh? You think Babylon boy can do me anything? Any whey night catch I is whey I lay I head!"

As my knees buckled under me and tears rolled down my cheeks, I saw a man wearing a white shirt, coming towards me. In a flash he was at my side. He grabbed my shoulders and said, "Sharon! Didn't I tell you not to come down here to me?" I quickly realized that I did not know him; he was trying to rescue me. I threw myself on him and wailed. I knew that God had sent me an angel. The men backed off and one said "a didn't know a you girl, she miss it by the skin a er teet". The "angel" half lifted, half dragged me off the bridge into the ghetto where a little scrawny dog attacked me. I ran and almost fell into a big, gully full of garbage.

When we were safe from the dog, and the abusers, my savior said "You don't remember me?" I looked at him closely through tear-stained eyes but his face vaguely looked familiar. He said, "You live up at the big house with the ole heap a mango trees and every time we pass, when we go play football and you see us, you would bring out a basket full a mangoes for us". That I remembered clearly! Mangoes were everywhere; rotting under the trees. I often wished I could send them to my family. Instead I picked them up and gave them to people as they passed. "What you doing in here?" I told him I was looking for Ms. Icilda. He took me to her house.

When Icilda saw me, and heard the story, she started to cry and her children started crying too. They said that the guys I encountered were murderers. I thanked the nice young man. Icilda took me to a shop just outside the ghetto and told me if ever I needed to reach her just leave a message there, never, never come back into the ghetto.

She accompanied me back to the house and when mom heard my ordeal she was brought to tears. I looked on silently, and then I said, "All is well that ends well!" After all, God sent me an angel!

That night as I played the day's events over and over in my head, I realized that it was because of my kindness that that nice young man went out of his way to help me. Kindness cannot be given away, I thought, it will always return to you.

Losing Mom

Mom's two daughters, Aunt Betty and Aunt June, who lived in Brooklyn, NY, took care of all our needs. They hired a nurse to take care of Mom during the daytime, while Jackie and I took care of her at nights.

At first, Mom would not allow us to tidy her when she wetted the bed or had a bowel movement. She would close her legs and feebly protested that it could wait until the nurse arrived next morning. She was too weak to fight us and finally, she gave in. We kept her clean at nights and the nurse cared for her during the daytime. Mom never had a bed sore and was never without a visitor. People came from everywhere to visit her and prayed with her; she was well loved. My mother and father also came to visit her and I was ecstatic to see them!

I was in the sixth form and majoring in business, against the wishes of my teachers. They thought I was better suited to major in science. I knew that mom was dying and I would be on my own soon, so I wanted to major in a field that would enable me to get a job quickly.

To assist with the finances, Mom had sublet one side of the house to students from the nearby Shortwood Teachers' College.

Aunt Lorrette, mom's very good friend, whom I came to love dearly, had two beautiful daughters, Carlene and Lorna. They were very kind to Jackie and me and would regularly give us their used clothing. Carlene had a boarder, a student from Antigua, Giselle, who was attending the College of Arts Science and Technology. We became great friends. I shared with

Giselle my desire to acquire a job before Mom passed because I was afraid of what the future would hold, without her being around. During my last few months in school, Giselle helped me develop my resume which I distributed to every major bank in Kingston. In Jamaica, banking is a prestigious profession and I did not want anything less. I was typing at 110 words per minute and taking shorthand at approximately 90 words per minute; I was confident that I would not have any difficulty acquiring a job quickly.

On my last day at Wolmer's, I received a letter from the Royal Bank of Canada inviting me to attend an interview on the following Monday. I panicked, as I did not have any clothing suitable to be worn to an interview. My friend, Giselle, outfitted me in her lovely red dress, and loaned me a handbag, and off I went for the interview which went well. I got the job! Mom was happy for me and between rests she said, "I wish that I could see how you turn out but I know that you are going to be alright. You have a good heart and you are always thinking about others. God is going to look down on you and say, Sandy is too busy caring for others to take care of herself, so I will have to take care of her. Yes, you are going to do just fine!" Then she told me not to forget my family in the country, they loved me and just wanted the best for me. She also made me promise to visit them as often as I could. Two weeks into the job Mom passed away; I was glad we had had this conversation.

The nurse told me she kept asking, when is Sandy coming home and she would tell her, around 5:30 p.m. Mom died at 4:45 p.m. I believe she was trying to hold on, waiting for me, but was too tired and had to go. I felt as though my heart was ripped from its mooring in my chest, and after the funeral director had left with her body, I curled up on her bed and cried myself to sleep.

On My Own

Approximately two weeks after Mom had passed, I returned home from work to find Jackie sitting on the verandah. She said her key wouldn't unlock the door; it appeared as though the locks had been changed. I too, was unable to get into the house. Together we sat there in shock, pondering what to do next, when uncle Chicadee rolled up in his big skylark and said, "Father Christmas dead and uno ave to find somewhere to go; uno can tek care a house? I could not speak, tears burned the back of my eyes but I refused to let them fall. I could not believe that we would be treated with such little respect. This was our home! He opened the door and told us to get our things and that we should be out by the next day.

We entered the house and saw that it was stripped bare; no paintings on the walls, no fine china and cutlery, except for two plates, two glasses, two spoons and two forks. The furniture that remained stood bare, and the beautiful crystal vase that cast a rainbow of colors with the sunsets, was no longer there. It was as though the light was taken from the house; after mom died the house had died too. I felt fear, but more strongly I felt wronged and I vowed not to spend another day there. I told Jackie to go to her father. Knowing he didn't care for me, I was going to find somewhere else to go.

Like a crazed woman, I pulled my clothing and shoes from the closet and tied them in a bundle. I thanked God for giving me a job and I knew that I had to make it to work the next day. I thought of a cousin who once lived with us while she was attending high school, and who now lived in a flat in Mona while she was studying at the

University of the West Indies. I knew she would welcome me until I could find myself a room.

I placed my belongings on the verandah chair and went out to the roadside to beg a ride from passing motorists. I flagged down a car and the driver stopped. He was an old man who said, "Get in!" I shook my head and said, "Reverse, I have some things for you to carry." He responded, "What a nerve you got eh!" But when he saw my face, he knew something was seriously wrong and he reversed the car onto the driveway. I threw my clothes on the back seat and asked him to take me to Mona. I am sure he was not going in that direction but somehow he could not refuse me and we drove in silence for the most part. He tried to pry, but I was not in the mood to talk.

When we arrived at June's flat, the gate was closed and it appeared no one was at home. I thanked the nice old man and threw my clothes on the sidewalk and sat on them waiting for June to come home. The man was distressed, "I can't leave you here like this," he said, looking very worried. I insisted that I would be fine. He handed me a business card and told me if there was anything he could do for me, please call. I looked at the card and realized that he was a medical doctor.

Shortly afterwards, June showed up with her boyfriend, and immediately she knew that something terrible had happened. They helped me gather up my belongings and ushered me into the small one bedroom flat. She gave me something to eat and offered me the cot in the living room. I apologized for imposing on her but I had nowhere else to go. I could not go home to Portland because I had a job in the city and I had to be at work by the next morning. I told her I would be looking for a room and hoped to be out of her apartment as soon as possible.

The next day, while at work, I inquired if anyone knew where I could get a room for rent. One lady, Sonia Phillips, said she could rent me her daughter, Natalie's room, as she was leaving for Miami to undergo surgery, and would be away for several months. I moved to Meadowbrook and spent many years with Sonia, Willie, Checke and Natalie. They treated me like family.

Accident

In keeping my promise to Mom, I visited my family in Portland every opportunity I got. I spent every Christmas and every Easter with them and they were all always very excited when I visited, bearing lots of food and goodies.

One day, while I was still living with my cousin, June, in Mona, I told her that I was planning to visit my family that weekend. June told me that she knew a Chinese man from Fairy Hill, named Eddie, who would go to Portland to visit his family every weekend, but he would drive through Junction. She suggested I get a ride with him and then take a bus from Port Antonio, only fourteen miles away from Upper Fair Prospect where my family lived. I thought that was a lovely idea and she contacted Eddie to ask for a ride for me. Eddie welcomed the company and said he would pick me up early Saturday morning.

By Friday evening I no longer had the urge to go to Portland, that weekend. I had a strong feeling that I should not take that trip! June and I tried to reach Eddie to tell him not to pick me up next morning but we could not reach him via telephone. He had no answering machine; we could not leave him a message. We tried to reach him several times during the night, with no luck. The early morning brought with it a heavy down pour of rain and Eddie in a white, open-back truck. Considering he came out of his way, I did not have the heart to tell him I did not feel like going, so I quickly grabbed my bags and off we went.

For the most part, the journey was uneventful. Traffic was light but the rain made the already bad roads treacherous. As Eddie navigated the many potholes, I sat tense, holding on to the edge of my seat, afraid that he might miss and send us over the cliff and into the deep ravines which lined the sides of the Junction road. After all, it was dark! Except for the car light, there were no lights on the road. Eddie proved to be a very skilled driver who knew this route well and I eventually relaxed as we neared Port Antonio. Eddie said he was going to stop at his house first and would then give me a ride home; I did not have to take a bus from Port Antonio.

As the morning broke, we drove through Port Antonio and headed toward Fairy Hill. The cool morning air caressed my face and I watched the sleeping town slowly come to life. The big orange sun was just slowly rising above the blue mountain peak when I felt a feeling of impending danger; my hair stood on ends and I broke out in a cold sweat. "Stop! Please Eddie stop!" I begged turning to look at him. "We are almost home. You wah pee?" "No! Please stop, just stop right now, just stop the truck!" Eddie pulled to the side of the road and said "Ok, mam, tell me when you ready" I looked around. We had just pulled through Drapers and stopped before entering the Sand Sand highway. I looked past Eddie, slumped back in his seat with his eyes closed, over the cliff and out to sea as if looking for answers, but none came. Eddie opened his eyes and saw someone he knew. After they had been chatting for a little while, he turned to me and asked, "You ready now, mam?" I didn't know what else to do so I said, "Yes."

The moment Eddie started forward he knew something was wrong. He turned to me with a terrified face, and said, "Sandy, I can't control the truck!" My mouth flew open as the truck swerved from one side of the road to the next. When Eddie steered one way the truck went the other way, and over the cliff we went. I braced myself for the crash by pushing my right shin on the dash board and I screamed as we crashed into a hill.

The truck turned on its left side dumping me on top of Eddie! I opened my eyes, I was alive!

Except for a burning sensation in my right shin, I was not seriously hurt. As I tried to get myself off Eddie, who was not moving, I saw a white man sliding quickly down the embankment towards us. He pulled me from the truck and placed me on the dew-filled brush then went back for Eddie. Like ants out of an anthill people including Eddie's brother, came from everywhere. I looked at Eddie, he had a concussion and his hair was matted with blood. He was placed in a car and taken to the hospital. I told Eddie's brother that I was not hurt and would like to go to see Eddie. He took me to the hospital and no doctor was there; it was too early.

Eddie was lying on a stretcher out in the hallway, looking like a wreck. I panicked and begged them to take him to the doctor's house. They knew where the doctor lived and we took Eddie there. I am not sure what treatment Eddie received but he came out walking. With his bandaged head he came directly to me and asked, "Sandy, what the hell was that? You know you saved our lives! If we hadn't made that stop, the speed at which we were going, we would be dead!" I was speechless!

I realized then and there that I was not supposed to be in the truck with Eddie. Yet, Eddie might have died if he was alone. Who or what was trying to save me? Why did I feel the way I felt before the accident? Why did I not feel like going that weekend? These and many more questions I could not answer, but of one thing I was sure, someone was watching over me!

Mas H

What did I know about love. I was only eleven years old. Call it what you will, puppy love, or school girl crush, Someone found me cute and I liked it! He was Mas H, Cracky Nut's son.

We were both attending the Fair Prospect Secondary School. I was in grade seven and he was in grade eight. He was the neatest boy in school and he walked with confidence and style. I had no idea that he ever noticed me, until one day while I was waiting in line, under the big fig tree, to buy patties for lunch, Mas H smiled, handed me a patty and said, "I already got you one." That is how it all started!

After school he walked me home and carried my books, even though he lived in the opposite direction.

Smitten with the attention, I grinned and giggled, and plucked leaves from the bushes on the side of the road all the way home. For fear of my father seeing us, we said goodbye at Miss Naomi's gate. One weekend he came to visit and outside under cover of early dusk, we attempted to kiss. I closed my eyes and the next thing I knew his nose was in my mouth. I spat and ran inside! That was the closest I ever came to a kiss and that was the end of my brief school girl's crush. I was too embarrassed, and I never spoke with him again.

Six years later, my sister, Pam, who was working at a haberdashery in downtown, Kingston, told me that she saw my old boyfriend walking naked on King Street. Upon hearing this news, I became highly distressed and walked all over downtown looking for him. I couldn't believe it! That nice, neat boy with the confident walk! I had to see for myself as she might have been mistaken! She insisted it was him.

True enough, one day I happened upon him walking down King Street. His hair was matted with dirt! He was filthy, naked, and emaciated. His long, flaccid penis lopped from side to side as he walked, rummaging into garbage cans looking for food.

I stood frozen, mouth wide open. Not my Mas H! Oh, my God! I had no food with me so I searched around in my handbag and handed him a dollar. He took it, looked at it, and then threw it away. Stupid me, what is a mad man going to do with a dollar? I followed him and called his name. He looked through me and did not appear to have recognized his name; he kept on rummaging through the garbage for food. I ran to a food stand and bought some food. When I caught up with him and handed him the food, he took it, without saying a word, and walked away, eating. He knows food, I thought, but he doesn't remember me, his one time girlfriend!

Still in a daze, I met with my sister who said she found out that he was a very talented artist and he was awarded a scholarship to study at The Institute of Arts and Technology. It was there that he suffered a nervous breakdown.

To this day, I still experience profound emotions whenever I see a homeless or a mentally ill person; all because of the indelible impression left on me by the destruction of the boy with the confident style!

Bruck Hand Sandy

"Me ungry!", "Eat congry", Jean, my older sister, responded. "Atla lef sardine an bread fe you fe give we!" I screamed angrily while slapping her on her arm. She sprung up from the verandah bench and charged at me like a bull. Younger and swifter, I got away and ran to the back of the house. I sat barefooted and starving on my grandfather, Tata's grave, crying and watching out for Jean to appear.

Chico, my father, was in the field and Atla, my mother, went to the airport to meet her cousin. Jean was left in charge. She wallowed in this privilege and got back at us for every little thing we had done to her. Responding to my growling stomach, I decided to pick a grapefruit but the tree was beside the verandah where

Jean was sitting with a whip waiting for me. I took a knife from the outside kitchen behind our small three bedroom house, to peel the grapefruit, and of course, to harm myself if necessary; however, I had no intention of hurting my sister with the knife.

I crept along the side of the house and started up the tree with the knife in my hand. The "monster" saw me and charged! I hurried up the tree and she came right up behind me. In a panic, I contemplated jumping from the tree, but was too high off the ground so I decided to cross over to an adjacent tree whose branches were intertwined. Though only eight years old, I had done this a thousand times with no difficulty, but today, I was being chased and I had a knife in my hand. The next thing I knew, I was flying through the air, hurling towards the ground. I threw the knife away so that I would not fall on it, and landed on my right hand, which snapped at the wrist!

As I howled and twisted in pain, Rose and Carol, our next door neighbors, rushed over. Jean hurried down from the grapefruit tree, and my father, who was just coming in from his field, tired and hungry, rushed to see what was wrong. When he saw my broken hand, he said in anger and frustration, "ole er mek me chap off er ras han". Rose and Carol held Chico pleading, "No Chico, no chap ar! No chap ar!"

My father eventually calmed down and flagged down Burkey's old truck for a ride to the hospital. He helped me up into the back of the truck. Two goats and a sheep were lying on banana leaves and each time I cried, the goats would respond, "m-a-a-y!" Dirty, tired, and very hungry, we arrived in Port Antonio and then had to walk a mile, uphill, to the hospital. I was given an injection and asked to count to ten. I didn't make it to seven. When I awoke in the hospital the next morning a cast was on my right hand, which was placed in a sling.

There was a big ship in the harbor. I was excited to see it!

Just before my mother arrived to take me home, a handsome sailor with blue eyes and wearing uniform, brought ice cream for all the children on the ward. He gave me two scoops. I slowly licked my tasty treat, while watching the big ship in the harbor, and thought of all the stories I would be sharing with my brothers and sisters. It has been almost 45 years, but I remember it as though it were yesterday; Jean, my beloved father, and that kind sailor from a distant land.

My Beloved Father

"**A**gua," he whispered. Beads of perspiration glistened on his forehead and his eyes, once sparkling with life, were now dull and distant. My mother hurried to get him some water, and I watched helplessly as my father lay dying on an old kayah mattress in the back room of our small three bedroom house; dying of complications from pneumonia, heart disease and diabetes. She held his head and placed an enamel mug to his parched lips. He sipped weakly.

He had not swallowed more than two spoonfuls when he choked, triggering a series of coughs. Water and phlegm flew from his mouth and sprinkled his family who were crowded in the tiny room. I didn't notice the glob of yellow snot that landed on my arm. I was listening intensely to that horrible sound that emanated from his chest. "Craw, craw, craw!" Is that the death rattle I have often heard people speak about! I had no idea, but whatever it was that possessed his once beautiful body, was now sucking the life from my beloved father.

My father was born in Cuba and came to Jamaica at the age of nine, with my grandparents, Vasco Berry and Charlotte Perry. He never learned to read and write English but he came to learn patois our native language. Now that he lay dying, he regressed to his childhood as a little Cuban boy, and he spoke mostly Spanish. As I stood helplessly watching my father, my heart full, my eyes clouded over with tears, his eyes came to rest on my face. Oh, my father recognized me, so I thought!

I was sent to live with relatives in Kingston when I was twelve years old and now I stood before him at age 24, elegant and sophisticated. I held my breath, my father recognized me! Then, he spoke and there was no doubt about what he said, "I want no strangers in this room". He looked directly at me and in a commanding tone he said, "Get out!" My heart broke in a thousand pieces and I sunk to my knees and wept.

My brother Carl tried to explain to him who I was. He never understood! He repeated it. "I said I do not want any strangers in this room!" I ran from the room. My father died, and he did not recognize me.

America Bound

I rented a three bedroom house in Edgewater and invited my older sister, Pam, her husband Paul and their son, Junior (Noel) to live with me. We got along fine and Marie Avenue became home. It was my last address before I emigrated to the U.S.A.

My cousin had brought an American with him to Jamaica on vacation, and they were guests in our home. This man, Thomas Potts, fell in love with me and asked me to marry him. I must admit, I wasn't sure whether I was in love or just infatuated, but knowing it was a sure ticket to get to the land of milk and honey, I said yes. I invited my boss and some friends, who worked with me at the bank, to witness my wedding at a little church off

Molynes Road. The following year I emigrated to America!

There is a saying in Jamaica, "See me and come live with me are two different things." Mom always said, "Two bulls can't rule in one pen!" The true meaning of these sayings became clear to me when I tried to live with Thomas. He was difficult to live with and I knew that I would not flourish under his thumb; so I moved to New York and lived on Linden Boulevard with Mom's daughter, Aunt Betty.

My first job was at Williamsburg Bank, and I realized that having a bank job in America didn't hold the same prestige that it held in Jamaica. I left the job, to attend Blake Business School in Union Square, Manhattan, where I graduated as valedictorian. My auntie, and Francis, my friend, attended my graduation ceremony. Thomas sent a dozen red roses but he didn't show up. I interviewed for three jobs in one day and received offers from all three. I chose the one which offered the highest pay, PaineWebber, an investment bank. Using my first pay check, I divorced Thomas Potts. We have remained friends, from a distance.

Life in the USA

While working at PaineWebber, I met Wendell Johnson at Emily's restaurant in Harlem in 1992. We moved in together and had our only child, Christopher, in 1995. By the time Christopher was two years old we were living in our own home in Peekskill, New York.

I worked with Charles Santos-Buch at PaineWebber, and when the company was downsizing Charlie accepted a job with Union Bank of Switzerland and took me along as his assistant. Charlie and I worked together, for seven years, in the private equity division of the company, UBS Capital, LLC.

In 1999 my mother was diagnosed with colon cancer. After the surgery, she wore a colostomy bag for one year. Due to lack of health insurance, she was unable to avail herself of chemo or radiation treatment in the United States, and consequently returned to Jamaica in 2001.

After September 11, 2001, the stock market and financial markets were experiencing difficult times; they lost billions of dollars. UBS Capital dwindled to just a few key employees and a decision was made to move into a smaller building in Greenwich, Connecticut. I decided, then, that it was time to leave New York.

I left my job at UBS Capital in 2002 and we sold our New York home. My husband, Wendell (Weejay) had taken a job in Nassau, Bahamas so I headed south alone and ended up in Griffin, Georgia. I moved into the house I purchased from my late Uncle John's estate. Christopher lived in the Bahamas with Weejay for one year until the renovations to the house were completed.

He returned and started the fourth grade and I enrolled in nursing school at Gordon College.

I graduated with an associate's degree in nursing in May of 2007 and took a job at Spalding Regional Hospital. In 2010 I returned to Gordon College to pursue my baccalaureate degree in nursing. I graduated cum laude on May 12, 2012 with a Bachelor of Science degree in nursing…..my new profession!

The Strength I Saw In One Who Could Not See

I was watching from the upstairs living room window as the ambulance pulled up and the driver helped her out. I saw her groping in her purse and assumed she was searching for her keys but to my surprise she came up with a pair of earrings which I had clipped on her ears earlier that morning. She clipped them back on her ears, retrieved her key from her purse, and let herself into the house.

As she fumbled her way up the stairs she shouted, "Sandy, are you in, dear?" I walked to the top of the stairs and acknowledged that I was. "Well! Well!" she exclaimed, "Lester had a good laugh when he saw me this morning. He said I looked as though I had just stepped right out of Hollywood."

I smiled, still marveling at how mentally strong she was! How could she maintain such calm, serene, state of mind when her whole body was falling apart, literally falling apart. She lost her eyesight at age 40; at that time she was living with only one kidney. By the time she was 42 years old, her second kidney collapsed and she had to undergo dialysis three times each week. She had to eat special meals at specific times, and she stayed alone in the house in the dark. My God! What a life! I thought, if she could only see my face, she would laugh at my expression of total bewilderment; she kept on, smiling…..always.

The two most distinctive characteristics about her were her radiant smile and her infectious laughter. I can still hear her laughing even now, a loud peal of happiness. Ironically, she found happiness in the fact that she was alive, something I took for granted. It struck me then while watching her fumbling her way up the stairs that I had to help make every remaining moment of her life happy. What I did not know was that my first two days in the United States, would be her last two days of being conscious.

That first night she offered me the guest room, but I refused and jumped into her bed with her. We stayed up until the wee hours of the morning, talking of old times, of people we knew, of any old thing, just talking and enjoying each other's company. She laughed a lot and told me I have always made her so very happy; this gave me great satisfaction.

The next day, she had a doctor's appointment so I gave her a manicure and a pedicure, shampooed and braided her hair and dressed her in a beautiful outfit with matching earrings. While she was at the hospital, I cleaned the house and made her a very special lunch.

When she returned, she slept for a few hours and when she awoke, she had me replace all the things I had moved around while cleaning. I had forgotten that she was blind and she had to memorize where things were. For the rest of the day we worked on some crossword puzzles. I would read and she would tell me the answers. She was truly elated, as solving crossword puzzles had become one of her favorite pastime activities over the years.

Again, we stayed up late, gossiping, and enjoying each other's company. The next day, after a very special breakfast, we worked on more puzzles and I told her of my dreams and aspirations. The day went by all too quickly, night came too soon and I had to leave. I felt a lump in my throat. In two days I had become so close to her it was very painful to leave. She told me to turn the lights out as I leave and when I did, my eyes welled up with tears; I was leaving a very sick person all alone in the dark. I turned the lights back on and left.

The following day, I received a call from her sister, Aunt Betty, informing me that she found Aunt June in the bathroom in a coma and she had been taken to the hospital. I returned to give what support I could and for two weeks we visited her every day. We kept talking to her hoping she could hear us, but she never regained consciousness. She passed away on November 14, 1987.

At the wake, a lady made her way through the crowd, asking for Sandy Potts. When she located me, she hugged and kissed me, and told me thanks for helping to make the last days of her best friend's life, happy. She said that the last words Aunt June spoke were about the wonderful weekend she had and how very happy I had made her. The tears came again; I had made a difference in her life!

That night I dreamt of her laughing, her distinctive laugh. I woke up, with a smile.

To Have Eyes but Not See

One bitterly cold day in the winter of 1989, I stood on the platform of the Church Avenue train station in Brooklyn, New York, anxiously awaiting a train to Manhattan. A Q train rolled into the station and I noticed that the first car was less crowded so I ran towards the front, thankful for a little room in which to read while en route. I entered the train and the doors closed promptly behind me.

The stench of rotting flesh was alive in the air. I didn't have to look to tell where it came from; the few commuters were bumping into each other at one end of the car. Unconsciously, I sat directly across from what, at a glance, looked like a discarded bundle. I felt ashamed to join the group at the other end of the car. I felt it was ungodly to scorn another human being no matter what his station in life, so I tried to make the best of the situation.

I took out my book and attempted to read. I read and reread the same page over and over; I couldn't concentrate. My every sinew, bone, and nerve was aware of this unfortunate person across from me. I heard a voice inside my head say, "There is none as blind as those who have eyes but refuse to see", and I blushed with shame that I could not bring myself to look. I thought of all the Bible stories I had read of the Good Samaritan; of Jesus healing the lepers. He was not afraid to touch them but I was afraid to even look. I sat there tasting his offensive smell seeping into my being, mixing with my phlegm and my blood, making me want to run out of the train at the next stop, to vomit.

I sat in my seat with my head bowed, feeling ashamed of myself for being so haughty. After a while, out of curiosity and shame, I slowly forced myself to look. First, at the people squashed together at the other end of the car, who like myself struggled to ignore the situation, making belief that they were elsewhere. Their expressions made me want to alienate myself from those who felt they were too good to stand two feet away from a person who is obviously in need of help.

Then I looked. He was lying across three seats, wearing layers and layers of old clothing, and on his head he wore a dirty turban. His feet were partially covered with plastic and paper bags and I noticed that his ten toes were missing. What remained was a mass of watering sores, which were obviously the source of the stench. He appeared very cold, and constantly rubbed his hands together for warmth.

As if he felt me staring at him, he turned his head to look at me and we were drawn into a silent conversation. He was challenging me. He asked, "How would you like to change places with me. To wander aimlessly day after day eating meals salvaged from garbage cans, sleeping on street corners and in train stations, constantly, in an attempt to avoid the bites of Mr. Frost, to never feel the warmth of a fireside or a well-filled plate, to be spat upon, scorned, cuffed, kicked and hated? How would you like to change places for just one day?"

In this sick, homeless man, I saw my father, my brother, my friend, and then I saw me! I shivered and broke out in cold sweat. "I never want to be you for one moment," I silently replied, and then I tore my gaze away.

I finally reached my stop and fled. Away from the stench, away from the site, but I could not run away from me. He was with me throughout the day. When I tried to eat I saw him begging for food, when I went for my coat, I remembered he had no shoes, no gloves, no coat, and when I went to bed that night, I wondered where he was laying his head.

There is none so blind as those who have eyes yet refuse to see. There is none so heartless as those who can help and refuse to do so.

An Embarrassing Moment

Have you ever been so embarrassed you wished the floor would open up and swallow you? Well, I have. During my first two years in the United States of America, I attended Blake Business School in Union Square, Manhattan, where I was trained to become an executive assistant. I applied myself well, and at the end of two years, I graduated with a 4.0 GPA. Graduation was postponed until two months after the course ended so I went to Jamaica on vacation.

Upon my return to the States, I found a notification from my school informing me that I was the valedictorian of my class and was expected to make a speech at graduation. I had only three days to prepare and practice the speech. I did the best I could, not knowing how to write a speech and the few friends I had were not of much help. I decided to memorize my speech.

On the day of graduation, I walked up to the podium, a proud student, feeling certain I would deliver my speech eloquently, and make my aunt, who was the only relative I had present, proud. I started out with a bang. I addressed the student body, members of the faculty and the guests and gave the necessary thanks and appreciation. I had incorporated a tribute to my aunt in the middle of my speech, at that point, I said, "To my wonderful aunt who has tolerated my negligence in house duties while I struggled to achieve this goal, your patience will not go unrewarded."

To my surprise, my aunt, who was sitting in the middle of the audience, stood up and blew me kisses and said, "I love you baby and I am proud of you!" This pleased the crowd immensely, especially the older folks who clapped loudly and cheered. When the applause ceased, my mind went blank. I didn't know what caused it, perhaps the shock of my aunt getting up and surprising me; but I had a mental block and could not remember another word of my speech.

As I struggled to remember my next lines, I stood there like a buffoon for what seemed like eternity. The audience went dead silent in anticipation of a conclusion. I became extremely nervous and perspiration trickled down my spine. My friend Lissette, noticing my predicament, came to the foot of the podium, and gently soothed me with positive reinforcement. I finally came out of the daze and said to the audience, "Thanks for your patience", and hurried off the stage to the ladies room, where my aunt consoled me. Feeling utterly embarrassed, I begged to leave. I couldn't face the questions and relive the shame.

That summer, I enrolled in "Speaking with Ease", a continuing education course at Brooklyn College, to help me overcome my fear of the stage. Since, then, I have not had many opportunities to speak to large crowds, but when I do, I deliver with utmost confidence.

A Gift is A Terrible Thing to Waste

I met Wendell Johnson at Emily's, a neat little southern style restaurant at the corner of 111th Street and Fifth Avenue in Manhattan, in the summer of 1992. The food was excellent and the music superb. It seemed that all who were present were enraptured by this handsome vocalist who captured the attention of all present, with his excellent singing. Wendell was a natural first tenor and his versatility allowed him to deliver from baritone to falsetto with equal strength and finesse.

It was a perfect setting, in which it should have been easy to relax. Instead, I was tense; his singing produced profound emotions in me. I sat at the edge of my chair peering into his mouth, waiting for the next note, the next song.

Not once during the four hours I sat there listening, was I disappointed. In fact, I was pleased, I was proud of him. This man was an extremely gifted singer and I felt honored to hear him sing.

On his break he met with the many patrons who congratulated him on his performance, and from his brief visit to my table, I noticed that not only was he a great entertainer, he was also very charming and personable. There was no place I would rather be at that moment, so I sat there, as if time did not matter, and enjoyed the entertainment.

It became apparent that I was not the only person who felt the magic of that perfect setting. Management asked the entertainer to take a break, hoping that some of the patrons would leave and make room for others who were waiting to be seated. As I sat there wrapped up in the performance of this truly gifted person, I asked myself, why is it that such a talented person is not known to the world? Then I thought of all the famous singers, and the stories they tell of their humble beginnings and I saw hope for Wendell Johnson, that one day soon he would get the recognition he deserves, for his exceptional talent.

Needless to say, I could not drag myself away until the entertainment was over, at which point I had a brief conversation with Mr. Johnson. He had been singing for over 18 years and I caught a glint of sadness in his eyes.

Although unspoken, I knew that his life was a difficult one. He knew he had to pay his dues to achieve his recognition. His will to continue performing was evidenced by the fact that he believed in the magic of his dreams.

I left the restaurant that night, feeling compelled to tell the world about him, and since then have been recommending people to stop by and hear him perform on Thursday and Saturday nights. After hearing Wendell Johnson sing, I was driven to support him in any way I could, because a gift is truly a terrible thing to waste.

My Love

I must admit that in the beginning I was simply trying something new. I had previously dated a Wall Street executive and had a grand time dining in the finest restaurants, enjoying performances on Broadway, and riding around in limousines. Every weekend provided an opportunity to do another fun thing in New York City with my date.

Unfortunately, this lifestyle wasn't making me happy. In fact, I felt as though, I was walking on eggs every day; afraid to be myself. Sometimes I wanted to shout, "I am just a little country girl with no family connections and no degree!" I continued to rub shoulders with the folks who graduated from prestigious universities and earned six figure incomes. I continued to date men who were afraid to take me home to meet their families. I knew that what I was experiencing could not be real love because I had to try too hard. I longed to just be myself!

I decided to change the direction of my life, so off I went to live with a man who found me irresistible, sexy, smart, and everything he had ever wanted in a woman. I was catered to, treated like a princess, chauffeur driven to and from my office, given countless floral arrangements and gifts for no specific reasons. Yes! I was catered to and loved by a big, handsome, tall stud of a man, who had no money, no degree and no connections. I wasn't pining for the life I left behind. I could walk around the house without bra, or fart without feeling embarrassed. I could let my hair down! But was I happy? I could not answer that question truthfully!

Many years later, I found myself selecting greeting cards with words that had meaning. I no longer had to select funny cards because I could not find cards that expressed my feelings. Now, I panic at the thought of losing my Weejay and I'm saddened when he complains of unrelieved back pains or other ailments. Yes, I have come to realize that like fine wine, love grows with age, with maturity, with time. Today, I look at my Weejay and I see a man who has aged almost completely grey, sagging skin, extra pounds around his mid section, and his once slight limp, now pronounced. I now see every imperfection as a scar of love and sacrifice for Christopher and me. I see a man who has never missed an important moment in our lives, who weeps when he has to be away from us. I see a man who is the personification of love and commitment. Yes, I have found a man who knows how to love and has taught me how to love.

Now, I can answer that age old question, "Are you happy? Finally, I can look in his dark brown eyes and lay my head on his shoulders. I can feel him in his songs. I can feel him when he is happy and when he's sad. Yes, my love, it wasn't love at first sight, but this love has weathered every storm and has withstood the test of time.

Speidy

For years we have held hands but for the first time I stiffened at Speidy's touch. A fleeting thought, people might think we are gay. I quickly pushed that thought away and held her hand. Through the streets of Manhattan we walked hand in hand, shopping and just as happy as we've always been with each other, in Jamaica, thousands of miles away.

Since the third form at Wolmer's High School for Girls in Kingston, Jamaica, we have been friends... and what a friendship! We were like two peas in a pod. We ate lunch together, we studied together, we visited each other's home. Her mother and father reminded me of my mother and father, and her brothers and sisters of my own brothers and sisters.

It was my firm belief that God gave me this family in Kingston to ease my longing for my own family, left behind in Portland. Little Marvin was the same age as my youngest brother, Jeff, and Brother P, the age of my brother Al. I loved Speidy's family and I knew they all loved me just as much.

Speidy, who now lives in Canada comes to New York every summer, to visit her in-laws, and of course, to see me. Whenever we would meet it was as though we had never been apart a day in our lives.

I often remember our first real boyfriends and all the emotions we shared because of those two boys; her Barry and my Mark. They are bitter sweet memories. I understand now that there is no love like a first love; we couldn't eat, couldn't sleep, and couldn't concentrate on anything at school. We were constant day dreamers and gigglers as we shared intimate secrets. When the news was good, we would hug each other and celebrate, and when things were bad, we would hug each other and cry. There was nothing we didn't share with each other; we were tight as white on rice!

Yet, over the years, there have been times when our friendship was challenged; but our amazing love for each other has brought us through those turbulent times and negative emotions. We have emerged stronger and more grounded in our friendship! I was the matron of honor at her wedding and we are godparents to each other's children. I must admit, although I have not been in touch as often as I would like, a Christmas has never passed without a word or a call from my sister friend.

My dearest friend Speidy, know that you and your family are never far from my heart and thoughts. You have been placed in my life not for a season, but forever, in my life, for a reason!

Aunt Lyn

This was my second time around the football field, and they were on their first, walking leisurely arm in arm; my mother and her sister, my Aunt Lyn, whom she had not seen for over forty-five years. I was sure they had much to talk about; forty-five years is a lifetime of memories. Aunt Lyn is my mother's only sister, who emigrated to England many years ago; they were now seeing each other for the first time in all those years!

In two separate worlds they each married and raised their families. My mother had ten children and my aunt Lyn had five. I can still see the family portrait of all my cousins hanging in our little house; Marcia, Ariane, Roger, Ricky, and Maxine. Yes, we knew them all by name and we looked forward to the letters which informed us about our relatives who lived so far away, in a place we could only read of or dream about.

After many years of unbroken correspondence, the letters stopped coming, and my mother became sad. She kept writing and writing but received no reply. After many unanswered letters she finally received a letter which informed us that our dear Aunt Lyn was ill. We also received the news that she had lost her husband, and her daughter, Marcia. We cried for our aunty who was so far away. I often saw my mother with one hand on her jaw, with a faraway look in her eyes, and I wondered, was she thinking about what's for dinner or was she thinking of her ailing sister and her family in that far away land. Will she ever see her sister again? My heart bled for my mother.

Several years after I emigrated to America. My mother came to live with us. As we huddled together one evening in our one bedroom apartment in the Bronx,

I once again saw that faraway look in her eyes, and I said to her, "As soon as I get us out of this one bedroom apartment into a house, the first thing I am going to do is send for Aunt Lyn to spend some time with you."…and I did!

Now, I watched my mother and her long lost sister, as they walked arm in arm, and it warmed my heart. My mother didn't talk much and she rarely smiled, but now, with her sister at her side, she wore a smile in her eyes; she was happy! I cried. Aunt Lyn stayed with us for three months and we were sad to see her go. Those three months had brought my mother immense happiness, which words could not express.

Within five years of this visit, my mother was back in Jamaica dying of colon cancer. My Aunt Lyn went to be with her. She spent every day at her sister's bedside, until she passed away. All my siblings had the opportunity to get to know Aunt Lyn, and they loved her, dearly! I know my mother died a happy woman.

The Last Time I Saw My Mother Alive

Cloaked in the dusky grey of the early dawn, my mother appeared ghostlike against the large oak tree that stood along the driveway of our home in Peekskill, New York. She was waiting for my husband, Wendell, to reverse the van out of the driveway. Today, my mother was being flown back to Jamaica to be with her husband and her other children. Though unspoken, we knew that we would never see her alive again.

I studied her as if to imprint a lasting picture in my mind. Her short curly hair appeared black in the dark, but I knew her hair was speckled with grey. Her cheekbones stood out like sentinels on her sunken face and her orange floral dress hung loosely on her small, frail shoulders. I moved closer to see her eyes, which were sad and fearful; not from fear of flying, but fear of the unknown.

Like a stab to the heart I suddenly realized, in that moment, that my mother knew that she would never see us again. I choked up and pulled her to my bosom. I kissed her cool cheeks softly, and she nestled close to my body like a tiny bird without wings, vulnerable and frail. I closed my arms around her as if to protect her, and I asked God to keep her in his care. Then my mother was gone.

I stood in the street and watched until the van was out of sight; until I could see or hear it no more. The tears came, and with them a flood of memories of my beloved mother; memories of her squashing chink all night to prevent them from sucking our blood while we slept…..memories of her hand on her cheek when she contemplated how to find food to feed us…..memories of her sitting silently in the midst of ten hungry, screaming children…..Memories of her telling us stories and jokes to sometimes calm us and at times scare us. Yes, they also brought memories of that dark day when she was diagnosed with colon cancer. How saddened and helpless we all were! Even after the tears had dried, the memories remained; countless memories of my beloved mother.

The Day My Mother Died

The day my mother died, November 7, 2001, I was working at UBS Capital on Park Avenue, New York. Since that last day when I held my mother, frail, and just a whisper of her normal self, I knew that this day would come. Yet, when the call came, I was not prepared for the emotions that overcame me. I screamed like a banshee and flung myself upon the ground, broken and in shambles as if hurled by a hurricane. Uncertain of what to do, my colleagues stood around silently. Finally, someone offered me some water and a town car was called to take me home. During my long ride up the Hudson River, I composed myself and reflected on my last conversation with my mother.

In her last days, my mother was unable, or too weak, to have a conversation. I asked that the phone be placed at her ears and I had spoken to her that morning just before she died. Aunt Lyn, my younger sister, Paula, Papa Zed, her husband, and her very best friend, Benjie, all stood vigil at her bedside. Through the phone, I could hear her heavy, labored, breathing and I knew she was traveling and would not be with us much longer.

At that moment, I said a prayer for my mother. I can't remember exactly what I said, but I asked the Lord to take away her pain and wipe away her tears. I asked him to take her home swiftly because she was hurting, she was tired, and she was ready. I asked Him to smooth the furrows from her brow, place her upon his bosom, and give her rest.

I am unsure whether my mother heard me, but that didn't concern me, I was praying not to her but for her. I heard her favorite song being sung by my family in the room, and I knew they were helping her make the journey. "Have thine own way Lord, Have thine own way. Thou art the potter and I am the clay. Mold me and make me, after thy will, while I am waiting yielded and still." As I listened to the singing and moaning in the room, I wondered if my father, my brother, Sherman, and all those who had passed on before, were there to meet her, and help her on her way. I couldn't resist asking this one last favor of my dying mother; I am sure she didn't mind. I asked her to tell my father about me, remind him of me. Tell him, my sister, Pam, has told me that he is always with her, that he comes to her in dreams, but I have never seen or dreamt of him. Please, mother, remind my beloved father of me.

Esther

It was not unusual for my friend, Esther, to shop for Christopher and me, she is the queen of shopping! When Wendell arrived home with an envelope from Esther, I became curious. I immediately opened it and was stunned to find a personal check in the amount of $5,000.00. Also in that envelope was a note which read, "To help you get that house in Georgia, Love Esther". I sat, speechless. Esther had been laid off and was presently trying to find a new job. How could she afford to lend me this money! I quickly dialed her number and thanked her for the amazingly generous gesture, but told her that my boss had just loaned me $10,000 that same day and that I had more than enough to get the house. If I ran into any unforeseen financial difficulties, I would let her know. That's the kind of friend my girl Esther is, generous, kind hearted, unselfish, and caring.

Esther and I first met at the apartment of her sister, Margaret. Esther and I were much closer in age, and quickly became close friends. It has been over twenty six years of friendship and while we have both experienced many major changes in our lives, our friendship has remained strong. Margaret died two years ago, and I saw my friend Esther, shattered and broken, at losing her sister. With the support of family and friends she gradually adjusted to life without Margaret.

Though, we now live many miles away, in separate states, Esther has not forgotten Christopher and me. Every Christmas, without fail, we can look forward to receiving a generous check and we say thank God for Esther, she has never forgotten us.

She has become a part of our family and she is included in every important family event. As I now gaze on my friend's photograph, which sits among my cherished memories, I think happy thoughts of my dear sweet Esther; that in a lifetime one can count true friends on one hand, and you my dear friend, are absolutely, hands down, one of the true, few.

As The World Turns

He would make his way to Annie's room, every morning and she would scoop him up in her arms and say, "Give me sugar, Chrisum, give me love!" Christopher would throw his arms around her neck and squeal with joy. Within the hour, he would be screaming his head off as we left for work, and Annie's heart would break, as it did every morning. She would linger, throwing kisses, telling him she would be back soon, and I would command her to let's get going he would get over it. She would say, "Geezum, I don't know how you do it!" To which I would reply, "You will understand, in time." For a year and a half we replayed this scene five days of the week, and then it was no more. Annie had left!

Annie was falling into depression. We were all worried. She had gone to Paralegal School and had graduated at the top of her class; however, she experienced difficulties in acquiring a job in Pennsylvania. She became cross and snappy.

One day I called her and asked if she would like to work in New York City, as my assistant, to gain some experience. She accepted, that's how my niece, Annie, came to live with us and work with me on Park Avenue for a year and a half. I taught her everything I knew. With her New York experience, she finally landed a job at a law firm in Reading, Pennsylvania, and moved back home. Christopher was devastated!

He was unable to express his loss and grief. Annie called frequently, and when Christopher recognized her voice he would hang up the phone promptly. We were stunned! Annie was his love, his life, and now he wouldn't give her the time of day. For years Christopher would not speak with Annie, but she never gave up trying. Years later when he was much older, he finally spoke with her.....and we cried.

Now, Annie has a son, Jordan, and she understands why she has to let him cry sometimes. When Michael, Jordan's dad, returned after being away for a while, Annie understood, perfectly, why Jordan did not have much to do with him.....and I smile, as the world turns!

Life in GA – Joyce & Granny

Life in Georgia is quiet. We live on a cul-de-sac, in a big, beautiful brick house surrounded by acres of woodland. To the rear of the property we have a large pond with fish of all types and a little stream that meanders its way through the woods and empties into the pond. The houses are far apart and the only interaction we have with our neighbors is when they drive by and wave when we are out in the yard. We have learned to love and appreciate what we have, and enjoy watching the many species of birds that frequent the fruit trees on the property or the grazing deer feeding on the grass around the pond at dusk.

When I am not gardening or cutting the lawn on a riding mower, I would sit for hours on the deck, over the water, and watch the fish and toads on lily pads, and the turtles as they sun themselves on the banks. Occasionally, a pair of geese would land on the water or a blue heron would stand for hours on one leg, waiting for an opportunity to snatch a fish. In the springtime, the squirrels would scurry away with the apples and the pears. At other times, I would attend my son's basketball games at his school. On one of those occasions, I sat beside a woman who I now count among my very special friends.

Joyce King, a retired educator, has a son, Brandon, who also plays basketball. Between cheers we chatted and exchanged phone numbers; that's how our friendship started. Joyce has shown me the meaning of Southern hospitality. I met her mother, Granny, who was the greatest cook and a champion at quilting. After months of going to games together, lunching and dining out, and visiting places of interest, Christopher and I officially became a part of Joyce's family. As such, we have been introduced to the other members of her family: sisters, aunts, uncles, cousins. We attend family barbecues, and there is always a place for us at the table every Thanksgiving and Christmas.

In 2011, the day after Thanksgiving, our beloved Granny died. We attended the service and burial and she is now resting beside her husband, in a little church plot in Talbot County, Georgia. Granny's passing has left a void in all our lives because she was truly a remarkable person. We will continue to cherish fond memories of her; a beloved mother, grandmother, sister, aunt and friend. Granny, may your soul rest in peace.

Christopher and Junior

He was very excited, and couldn't sleep, so I allowed him to stay up and wait. When Junior (Noel), and his friend finally arrived it was way past his bedtime, so Christopher greeted them briefly and went off to bed. The next morning when he left for school, they were asleep. That evening he couldn't wait to get home. When the school bus stopped, he burst through the doors like a bullet and stopped abruptly when he didn't see his cousin's vehicle in the drive way. His face fell and I watched as he ran quickly to the back of the house, thinking that the jeep might be parked in the rear. He was again disappointed and I opened the door and told him they had gone into Atlanta. My nephew, Junior, and his friend drove down from Pennsylvania to spend a week with us, or so we thought.

After his love affair with Annie, Junior was the next best thing for little Christopher. When we lived in New York, we often visited Junior in Pennsylvania. Christopher was always excited to see him. Junior was an exceptional kid. He was outstanding in every sport and often made the local news. We were always very proud to read the many articles written about him, and my sister, Pam, his mother, would clip them out of the newspaper and make scrapbooks.

When we visited them, we would enjoy going into the room of fame. Every space on the wall had trophies, certificates, ribbons, and medals; many of them gold. Junior once appeared on the front page of a magazine and we framed it. During his senior year in high school, he was crowned the home coming king; the only African American in the entire school was nominated the homecoming King. After high school he attended Bucknell University where he continued his stardom in athletics. We were all very proud of him, and Christopher, saw him as an inspiration and a role model.

They came home very late that night, after Christopher had gone to bed, and, again they were sleeping when he left for school that next morning. That evening, he didn't rush off the bus, he walked, and he didn't ask where they were, he simply sighed and put his book bag down. I knew his heart was heavy with disappointment. Being only eleven years old, Christopher was excited that his cousin was coming to spend some time with him. On the fourth day of returning home from school to the same disappointment, my son said, "Mom, I don't even remember what he looks like!" My heart was sad for him. I knew then I had to say something. When my nephew came home that night, after my Christopher had gone to sleep, I said, "Christopher said he doesn't remember what you look like." That was all I had to say, my nephew knew then what he had to do. Next day, he stayed at home and waited for Christopher to return home from school. When the bus pulled up at our gate, although I didn't see it, I knew my son's heart skipped a beat when he saw Junior's jeep in the driveway. He stopped for a second, looked at it, and then sped down the driveway. When he burst through the door I was happy to tell him that they were at the pond fishing, and Junior would like him to come on down so he could teach him how to fish.

He threw his bag down, changed his clothes quickly, and darted off to the pond. I watched them from the kitchen window as I prepared dinner, my nephew with his arms around my son teaching him how to fish, and I smiled.

That evening my son caught his very first fish and I ran for my camera to capture the moment. Although, I never placed that photo in a frame, I know my son, and my nephew, will never forget that day.

Now, many years later when I learned that my nephew had planned a "bonding day" with his nephew, Jordan, my heart again swells with pride. Noel has matured into a great husband and a devoted father, and he now knows that he is a role model for all the children in our family, and other families. He now knows the importance of spending time with the little people who hold him in very high regard.

Christopher

Atla, my mother, usually walked our son, Christopher, two blocks to Peekskill high school where he was taking swimming lessons, but today, she was not feeling well so Wendell and I took him. When we entered the pool room, we were surprised at how much older than Christopher the kids were. He was then, four years old, and the other kids all looked twice his age. Christopher did not appear to be intimidated by their size, and he confidently joined them in the pool.

The class began with the instructor requesting they race to the other end of the pool at the blow of a whistle. Wendell and I looked at each other and shrugged our shoulders, wondering if Christopher could swim the length of that gigantic pool; this was only his fourth lesson!

Nervously, we watched with abated breath, as the kids darted off, rapidly, leaving Christopher behind. Swiftly, they swam their way across the pool to the other side, and stood wet and wide-eyed, watching little Christopher, only half way across the big pool. Slowly, but confidently, one stroke at a time, Christopher swam towards his destination. We were amazed that he did not pull off to the side when he realized he was so far behind. Instead, he pressed on, and as Wendell and I cheered him on, everyone joined in, "Go Christopher, go! Go Christopher go!" After what seemed like eternity, Christopher finally reached his destination, and the room erupted in applause and cheers.

Proudly, Christopher pulled himself from the pool, and ran to us as the instructor approached and said, "I think your son came to the wrong class. He must belong to the class in the next building". Realizing our mistake, we gave a sigh of relief. We patted Christopher on his head and congratulated him on a great performance, then we headed to the other building feeling proud of a son who was filled with stamina and perseverance, the stuff of which great men are made.

Eleven years later, Christopher joined the cross country team at Pike County High School. He was the heaviest kid on the team, and finished last in every race, for the entire season. This did not stop him, he kept right on running. One day I asked him, "How do you feel about finishing last all the time?" He replied, "I am not in it to win, and my coach understands that. He encourages me to keep going and rest when I have to. But mom, when I first started running earlier this season I was clocking three miles in 45 minutes and was stopping numerous times. Now, I am doing the same three miles in 32 minutes, without stopping." I jumped up and kissed him and said, "Well done my son! I am proud of you!" to which he replied, "Some kids do it in

18 minutes". I pretended not to hear that! Then his dad, met with the trainer and asked him how Christopher was doing. He replied, "If all the kids were like Christopher, they would all be champions. He has the stuff great men are made of; stamina and perseverance!

Now in High School, and 45 pounds lighter, Christopher is the captain of an undefeated junior varsity team and he plays center mid on the varsity team. Our son, Christopher, the champion! He possesses the stuff of which great men are made!

College Friends

My three most memorable friends from college are Jeanine, Ismenia, and Brandie. They are as different as day and night; a Haitian, a Venezuelan, and an American.

Jeanine, my Haitian girlfriend, is a go-getter; a fighter! I admire her resourcefulness and above all, her warmth and kindness. Jeanine and I met in a math class at Gordon College in 2004, and we have been friends since then. She is married with two children and speaks French and English fluently. Although I cannot speak a word of French, sometimes, Jeanine speaks to me in French and I smile realizing she is so comfortable with me being around her, she forgets I do not understand her native language. A few years ago our families spent a vacation in the Bahamas, and we had a fantastic time. Jeanine and her family: Sylva, Sebastian, Samaria, and Dakota the dog, have become a special part of my life here in the South, and I thank God for them.

Ismenia, a beautiful Spanish lady from Venezuela, has been my inspiration throughout nursing school. She speaks English well, but with a Spanish accent. Nursing school was difficult; however, Ismenia was brilliant, and we watched many smart people drop out of the program. The most challenging task for Ismenia while in nursing school was writing papers. She overcame that too!

During our final semester of nursing school, I became ill, and had severe anemia as a result. I had no energy and could not retain anything I learned. My dear friend Ismenia, carried me through that last semester of school. When we studied she would read aloud and talk through the information and I would listen; she refused to let me drop out! We graduated on May 12, 2007 proud of our amazing achievement. Two days after graduation, I had a hysterectomy and two weeks later Ismenia and I took the State Board exam. We passed! Ismenia and I often meet for lunch and a movie.....our special friendship continues.

Brandie and I met in a Biology class when I returned to college to get my Bachelor of Science in Nursing (BSN) degree in 2010. We had a difficult professor, but I enjoyed Biology and was at the top of the class.

Brandie approached me one day during class, and asked if we could study together. I had told my sister that I would love to find a friend like Ismenia during my BSN program, but I wasn't looking because there is only one Ismenia. Brandie and I met every morning, Monday through Thursday to study in the library, for two hours, before our first class. I shared with her my well proven study techniques and she started making all "A's". We spent a year together and during this time we became close friends. She loves to ride and owns her own horse.

I saw Brandie experience all kinds of difficulties relating to social and financial problems. I sensed her loneliness and her fear, and I prayed for her. I was there when she lost her husband and I walked with her through the changes that resulted. I see her now with her two small children, happy, strong, and confident.

Although we hardly see each other anymore, every opportunity we get, we connect and enjoy each other's company. Brandie is becoming as dear to me as my other "forever" friends.

Me Auntie

"A feel good!" sang James Brown, and Me Auntie sprung up like a feline, from her chair by the pool side, with an "Ow!" This was Christmas 2006 in the Bahamas. Every head turned to watch this display of agility from a 70 year old "old lady."

My heart pounded in my chest in anticipation of Me Auntie falling into the pool; however, I remained rooted in my seat, shocked and amazed, not sure whether to be embarrassed or proud. Being half her age, I had an element of envy as I could not dance as well. It was spectacular to watch Me Auntie dancing to the music, not missing a beat and moving to the rhythm as if she was 20 years old.

For a moment, I thought that Me Auntie might've been drunk; but she had only just arrived at the party and was still on her first drink. No, Me Auntie wasn't drunk. Me Auntie could hold her liquor! This is the real Auntie, a party animal.

Feeling a bit useless, I nudged my brother, Al, who was standing beside me, and said, "Let's go dance and steal Auntie's thunder!" Al replied, "Me! Me naw go mek damn pappy show of me self. Mek Auntie gawn, she betta watch she no fall ina de pool." I could not stop laughing! The music continued and Me Auntie kept twirling. One brave tourist joined her on the floor; he was no match for her.

He was high as a kite or drunk. Possibly both! Moving to the sound of an imaginary music that only he could hear and Me Auntie made mince meat of him.

The song ended and the crowd erupted in a loud applause and individuals complimented Me Auntie on a terrific performance. Without the slightest bit of modesty, Me Auntie replied, "Oh shucks, you should have seen me in my prime!" Yes, a Me Auntie dat!

Weejay in the Everglades

Five year old Jordan held tightly to Michael's neck and cried for the entire fan boat ride through the Florida Everglades. I snapped pictures of turtles basking in the sun, alligators lurking under lily pads, and members of my family trying to enjoy the tour in spite of Jordan's griping and whining. Finally, the tour was over and Jordan was the first off the boat, dragging his mother, Annie, off the pier and up to the tuck shop to get him some ice cream and candy. Minutes later, Annie, Jordan, Christopher and I emerged licking ice-cream; that's when we became aware that we were missing Weejay and Michael. We looked towards the lake and saw Weejay as he accidentally stepped backwards off the edge of the pier, into the Everglades, with a loud splash.

Disturbed by the noise, two huge alligators which were basking on the far side of the everglades, slid quietly into the water. Shocked and stunted by this dramatic event, we stood motionless with our mouths agape, lick frozen in mid-air; waiting for the alligators to swallow Weejay. Everyone on the pier panicked, but no one jumped into the murky, alligator-infested water, to save him.

Weejay emerged almost immediately, like a swamp thing covered in muck and plant roots, screaming for help. His right hand held high above his head, tightly clasping his car key. In a flash, all the men on the pier grabbed him and pulled him from the Everglades. He was saved from the snapping jaws of the alligators, in the nick of time! It was only as he was rescued that we found our voices, and our feet, and ran to him. What do you say to a man who was just snatched from the jaws of swamp alligators? Nothing! We just laughed and laughed; we peed ourselves laughing. Yes, we were relieved that our Weejay was safe. After the danger had passed, we found the whole thing hilarious. For the first time, the man who usually finds a reason to laugh at everything was not laughing. He was angry! Angry that we laughed when he almost drowned or worse, was almost eaten alive by alligators. THAT'S NO LAUGHING MATTER!

Ava

Friends, since we were babies, my dear friend Ava, knows me well and I her. We shared in the joys of our only children: her daughter, Janine, my god daughter, and my son, Christopher, her godson! Strong willed and industrious, I watched my friend as she embarked on several projects to provide for her family. She had a gourmet restaurant and a catering business. These were profitable for a while, then under the strain of dwindling finances they eventually failed. Always forging ahead, she tried her hand at the next thing. Ava has been a mother and a father to her daughter, and has singlehandedly, put her through one of the best high schools, and then through college.

I have many fond memories of Ava and me way back when we were little girls. I was a tomboy and would climb up the apple tree like a piston while "Princess Ava" waited standing on the tombs below to catch the lovely ripe apples I would throw to her. I remembered she would rarely ever catch one, and we watched with disappointment as one by one they split on the eerie grey stones. Much later after we had both moved to the city, Ava and I took many trips to Portland together to visit our families. There were unforgettable moments when we dated two friends. Another cherished memory of us walking along Boston beach, collecting sea shells with Janine and Christopher, two friends, now all grown up and caring for two little people.

Ava's mother, Ms. Benjamin, was an excellent example of a caring and committed mother and Ava has followed in her footsteps. Though we now live in two separate cities, hundreds of miles apart, we have kept our friendship alive and have continued our strong relationship. Ava has faced many challenges, spiritually, and financially, but she has always found a way to overcome them all.

Years ago, Ava gave her life to the Lord and He now carries her load while she ministers. With God as her anchor, Ava has finally found peace. Ava my oldest, and one of my dearest friends, has cast all her cares at His feet.

Sister Doreen

I remember when you were lost, spiritually and financially lost, and I remember our many letters, trying to uplift, to inspire, to encourage. Three children to support on your own after the father of two of them had died. I remember your abstinence from sex and men, while you struggled to regain control of your life…and, I remember my pledge to you; for every letter you wrote updating me on my beloved family, I promised to reply quickly and enclose $20. Yes, I remember all too well the letters that never ceased to arrive. A steady stream to quench my thirst for a family once lost. Every dollar you received from me, always just in time, you saw as a blessing from God. To you, I was an instrument of God and that there was hope for you.

Yes, my sister, I remember when you wrote that you had found the Lord and He had sent you on a mission. Humbled, and afraid, you took your children to St. Thomas, but, your fear was not of man; your fear was of God! I remember the many testimonies of your experiences wrestling with the devil and also of your many testimonies of God placing people in your path to help you. As you grounded yourself in the Lord, and made Him your roots and your branches, you began to bear fruits. "For whosoever believeth in me shall not perish!" saith the Lord. You knew you were no longer lost. Giving glory to God, you asked for a husband and God gave you Morais, a young, handsome husband to support and stand by you as you cloaked yourself in the armor of God and continued his battle. Yes, my sister, Doreen, I remember when your children went astray and you fasted and prayed and the Lord answered your prayers and put your daughter, Terry-Ann in the hands of the church, and plucked your son, Addie, out of the jail.

As I see your life unfold before me, I see a common thread with mine. I remember my journey with him through the storm, when he snatched me from abusers, when he carried me when I was weary. Now, I face each day with confidence and courage, knowing that the same God, who is smiling on you, my sister Doreen, is also smiling on me!

Sonia

I was there from the beginning, sharing in the joys that a child brings to its mother through to the agonies brought by a defiant teenager. Mine have been the ears that listened, and the shoulders on which Sonia cried, when her beloved Joe died, unexpectedly; the loss shattered her life. I was there when her finances were low; and watched her pluck the hair from her head until she was almost bald.

But, I was also there when she found her now, beloved husband, Leroy, who has become an anchor in her life. I now hear her laughter and giggles instead of her cries and her pain. I now hear her plans for the future and share in her joys.

Recently, my lifelong friend who enjoys dressing up and going out, who enjoys buying nice things and giving gifts, who is happy when everyone is happy, is once again sad. Not saddened because she sees her daughter, Natalie, as a disappointment; although she repeatedly says that she is her biggest heartbreak. She is saddened because a lump has been found in her breast, a lump that could be cancerous!

After the initial shock, the fear and the tears, and with her friends and family praying for her, my friend moved forward and courageously, had a lumpectomy. Sonia is now undergoing chemotherapy and radiation treatments.

This time my friend's eyes are opened to the true meaning of life, to the things that are important. She now cherishes the love of a wonderful husband, of an only child and grandchildren; of family and friends, and my friend Sonia, says, Thank God for them! Thank God for life!

Not Today

I opened my eyes and turned my head towards the whispers. Weejay, Auntie, Pam, Doreen and Christopher were sitting at the window trying to keep their voices low. I looked at the clock on the wall and was shocked to see it was almost six thirty in the evening. I felt as though I had died and had now come back to life.

The last thing I remembered was that I was brought into the operating room at 8:00 a.m. Was I sleeping all that time! How long did the operation last? Then in walked my doctor who said, "You continue to amaze me!" I wasn't sure what he was talking about. He asked if I was in any pain. I told him I felt pain only when I tried to move. He advised me that in spite of the pain I must make every effort to get up and walk.

On Saturday, May 12, 2007 I graduated from nursing school and two days later I was a patient at Spalding Regional Hospital undergoing a hysterectomy. I had been bleeding and passing huge clots, nonstop for the past six months, and had become extremely anemic and weak. I spent three days in the hospital and saw my doctor so many times, I lost count! Later I found out the reason for his frequent visits.

My surgery was a total disaster! The doctor informed my family that he had expected the vessels that fed my fibroids to be the size of the lead in a pencil, instead the vessels were the size of the pencil! As a result, I had massive bleeding and almost bled out on the table. My uterus was the largest, ugliest uterus he had ever seen! He had to close me up as quickly as he could. In short, he was not comfortable with how the surgery went. Now I know why I felt as though I had died and came back to life. I now understood why he kept checking on me.

I reflected on my sister, Doreen, a minister, who felt she had to be here for my surgery. She had called a friend to see if she could get a buddy pass and he did not have any. Just as she was about to hang up the phone a co-worker walked by and said to her friend, "I have a pass you can use!" Doreen knew God wanted her to be at my bedside. She prayed and fasted before, during and after the surgery.....until I regained consciousness.

While death stood in the shadows on his pale white horse, waiting for the command to fetch me home, God gave the command, "Not today death, not today!"

Dancing With My Father

It was while dancing Zumba, that I remembered. First, a fleeting memory, then, it all came flooding back as I zumbaed in my living room to the fast-paced flamingo and cumbia rhythms. I recalled a time, decades ago, when I was a very small child, three or four years at the most. Yes, I clearly remembered dancing with my father as my mother prepared dinner for our family.

My father would attend to my little brother, Sherman, and me to prevent us from getting in her way as she moved around our small wooden kitchen.

She would usually scream for one of our older siblings to come take us away. But today, my father was entertaining us as she blew smoldering embers and busied herself about the kitchen. I could see it now, oh so clearly, the little battery operated radio my father brought from America when he returned from farm work. It was hanging on a nail with its antennas up like ears, smoked meat hanging from the rafters above the fire place, and smoke rising up to meet it!

That day my father had returned home from the field with a crocus bag filled with breadfruit, yam, cocoa, banana, cabbage and sugar cane and my mother was happy. She was happy because today we will all have plenty to eat! I would be lying if I tell you who was singing, and what song was playing on that little radio, but as clear as day, I remember my father dancing with me! While my tiny feet were on his, he held my hands and danced; moving to the right then to the left, while shaking his bottom and singing in Spanish. Yes, he was singing in Spanish even though I am sure it was reggae music playing. My father was reliving festive times in the streets of his native Havana.

Now, almost forty-eight years later, this precious memory fills me with joy, and I wish that I could dance with my father again.

Sherman

In 2012 in America, A young black boy, Trayvon Martin, was killed, while walking home from the store, by Mr. Zimmerman, a neighborhood watchman. At the time of his death, all he had in his hands were a bag of skittles and a can of ice tea. The 911 operator had told the watchman not to follow Trayvon, yet he did! Mr. Zimmerman claimed that he feared for his life and invoked the "Stand Your Ground Law". This story went viral because the killer was allowed to walk free without any investigation. The people in support of Trayvon Martin could not see how this law applied and felt that at the least, Mr. Zimmerman should have been held in custody and the shooting should have been investigated.

This incident took me back to Jamaica in 1989 when my younger brother, Sherman, was killed by police. It was alleged that he and some friends had picked coconuts from someone's property. Police, after arresting him, tied him up and beat him in an attempt to force him to give up the names of his friends who were alleged to be with him. He died in their custody. To cover up the murder, they strung him up in his cell and said he hung himself. Everyone who knew Sherman found this hard to believe, and the entire district protested. Hundreds of people blocked and lined the streets, crying out for justice.

The Prime Minister, Michael Manley, stopped Sherman's burial and ordered his body be brought to Kingston for an independent autopsy. The autopsy showed that he died from a blow to the back of his head and his arms were also broken in several places. Even with the protesting and the autopsy results, no arrest was made.

The police began to intimidate our family and the case was dropped for fear of our safety. No matter what action we took, it could not bring Sherman back; so we looked for a silver lining in this tragedy, to mitigate the pain and help us move forward. As a teaching moment for my two younger brothers and sister, I made a promise to them that I would finance whatever endeavor they undertook to develop a skill that would always enable them to support themselves. With constant encouragement and financial assistance, my younger sister, Paula, became a hair dresser. One brother, Jeff, became a carpenter and another, Al, became a mason.

I have found ways to mitigate the pain, and time has healed the wounds, but I still remember Sherman's captivating smile, his kindness and his love of children. My brother died a tragic death and similar incidents, when they occur, open the wounds once healed, and cause great pain to resurface. Though these two incidents occurred in two countries, hundreds of miles apart, I realize the more things change, the more they remain the same.

Giselle & Jerielle

Tall, elegant, and sophisticated my Antiguan friend, Giselle has been my mentor and role model since I was fifteen years old. She attended the College of Arts, Science and Technology in Jamaica (University of Technology) while I was still in high school. I admired the way she carried herself and her command of the English Language. She returned to Antigua and we stayed in touch and after I moved to the United States I visited her in Antigua and enjoyed a great time among her family and friends.

Giselle and her two children, Leslie and Jerielle, moved to Houston, Texas. Our friendship has remained strong throughout the years, and I have visited her, with my family, several times since she has been in the United States.

Early one morning, Giselle called to tell me her daughter, Jerielle, had written a paper about me, for a school assignment, and that she had to read it to me. Jerielle had to write about someone whom she admired and who she sees as a role model. I was pleasantly surprised. I have known Jerielle since she was born, and though separated by hundreds of miles, her mom and I have managed to keep our bond of friendship alive for a period greater than thirty-five years.

Unknown to us, Jerielle, was motivated by our friendship. She revealed in that paper, that all through her life, the only constant in her mother's life, outside of her family, was Auntie Sandy. She would hear us talk about the death of my father, my brother who was murdered, my mother's colon cancer diagnosis, and the day my mother died. She was listening when I called to inform her mom that we were selling our house in New York and moving to Georgia after September 11 had put the company out of business. She was listening when I enrolled in nursing school and when I graduated as a registered nurse in 2007. Yes, Jerielle was listening, admiring, and motivated, that for all the negative things that have happened to me, I could still find the strength and courage to go on, to pick myself up and achieve great things, "always with a smile", she said.

The paper was titled, "A Flower Can Grow From a Crack". As I listened, tears of joy rolled down my cheeks; all these years I have wondered, and searched for a purpose to my life. Today, a child has shown me that if I can touch a life positively, if I can motivate a person to be strong, if I can give someone hope, then my life has a purpose, my life is not in vain. Now, I share my stories. Jerielle, I share my lifetime memories because of you!

I Have Been Hurt

I have been hurt! I have been bruised and trampled upon many times. Each time I picked myself up, brushed myself off, and tried again, because I am worthy! One guy left me, resigned his job, moved, disconnected his phone and warned his friends and family never to give me his forwarding information. Yes, he left me broken and weeping for weeks, perhaps months. Left like a thief in the night after three years of invested emotions. Why? All because I was not ready to have his baby; I was building my career.

Another ended four years of what I thought was the perfect relationship because I told him that one day I would like to get married and have children. He on the other hand, said that he would never get married and didn't want any children. Yes, many more weeks and months of hurting but I insisted I am worthy to be loved so I tried again and again to prove that I am worthy to be loved and cherished.

I am no stranger to mental abuses. One love affair ended when my handsome Wall Street executive boyfriend decided to throw a party in his beautiful apartment to introduce me to his friends. He did not want to have it catered; he wanted to share a special recipe. On the day of the party he had me peeling potatoes and frying chicken all day when everyone else was out dolling up themselves in readiness for the party. I didn't make it to pick up my dress from the cleaners. My hair style flopped from me busying myself in the kitchen all day, and my manicure was ruined from peeling potatoes. The night was a disaster! My lover was disappointed with my appearance. Perhaps I should have tried a little harder to put myself together and get to the party late; but, it was supposed to be a party to introduce me to his friends so I was expected to be there when the first guest arrived.

When the doorbell rang, he hurried to get the door and greeted a tall, sexy girl whom he whisked off to the bar with barely a "This is Sandy" nod in my direction. To compound matters, when the doorbell rang again he said to the girl, would you please man the door for me, and the 'hottie' sassied on over to the door as though she was the mistress of the house. I shrunk a thousand times! His best friend, who was witnessing my humiliation, walked over to me. I burst into tears and begged him to please take me home. He did! I cried all the way and to add to my degradation my boyfriend did not miss me until the party ended; I guess that was when he was ready for my lanky legs to curl up with him in bed. That's when he called shouting, "Don't ever tell anyone that you are my girlfriend; you walked out of my party on me!" "Go jump off a cliff," I screamed! "You need to come and get your things out of my apartment," he commanded. "Burn them!" I shouted and hung up the phone. Then I wept and experienced the pain for weeks. I kept hope alive. I am worthy to be loved! At times like these I would transport myself to a time and place when I was happy, when I felt loved, and like an oasis in the desert my first love kept me sane. Thoughts of him kept alive the hope that I am worthy to be loved and cherished. I became highly motivated to succeed, to let them all regret they had treated me so poorly.

After decades, I lived to see the man who left me in the dead of night, twice married with two daughters; he came bawling with regrets, wanting to marry me. I told him that I was happily married and am the mother of a wonderful son. He cried because he had wanted a son. The man who had me cooking and ignored me at his party lost his eye sight and is now blind. I am sure now he would be happy to grope in the dark and feel me beside him. He wouldn't mind now if my nails weren't manicured and my hair a mess. Yes, I lived to receive a call from him from a hospital bed crying and expressing great regrets for dumping me. He said I was the most caring girl he has ever known and he knew I would not have deserted him when he needed me most. He was right about that. I would never have left him had he gone blind while we were together. I obliged him with a few phone calls to check on him while he was hospitalized. My caring nature couldn't help it; however, I never visited him. He couldn't see me, sophisticated lady that I had become, and I didn't want him to grope me, so I stayed away and allowed someone else to worry about him.

Life is what it is, some say, but I am going to make it what I want it to be! Half a century of disappointments and failed love affairs, have taught me some invaluable lessons and clarity is now mine. I see that the rest of my life should be spent on things that matter, and people who are important in my life. Today I live out the expression, "To thine own self be true." When giving love, I will give it with all my heart and soul because I want to, and hope that you, the recipient of my love, will appreciate it.

The Love of a Woman

Love, to me, was always fleeting and fragile; I couldn't grasp it, much less keep it. I know now that this is untrue. Love, I have discovered, is so immense it encompasses everything, it is everywhere, one just has to reach out and touch it. Whether it is love for a man, woman, or child, love is as much to the giver as the receiver. I know because I have discovered the love of a woman, a very special woman.

She opened her arms and her heart to me and I did not hesitate to lie upon her bosom and let her stroke my hair and call me precious. We need each other; she needs to be loved and cherished and so do I. We have formed a symbiotic association, a bond of love flowing back and forth, feeding and sustaining each other.

Like two beacons on a hill our love shines for the entire world to see, and there is no denying it. When I am with her, she giggles like a child and I am always happy to see her face light up like the morning sun. When we are apart, my heart saddens wondering, will I see her lovely face again? Frightened at the thought, I quickly made plans to visit. Without fail, she would ask each time we speak, "When will you be back, you bring so much light and energy when you are here; the house is not the same without you." When I am with her, I feel alive and free, a feeling so difficult to put into words, a feeling only hearts can feel.

I know that love has many faces and can be found in many places. I know because I found love in the arms of a remarkable woman, Miranda Cameron. I love you Mother! Peter, Mark, Susan, thanks for sharing your mother with me.....especially now, that my heart bleeds for the love of a mother.

Never Lonely

We have always shared a great sister relationship, but in the last ten years we have become very close friends. Ironically, the vast distance between us has brought Steiger (Pam) and me closer. The telephone has become a vital link in our now separate lives. With unlimited calling plan, we speak with each other almost every day of the year! What we find to talk about for hours is a question often asked. We don't just talk though; we keep each other's company too, at times without saying a word. Yes, over the phone! We place each other on the speaker and go about our daily tasks: cooking, washing, even weeding the garden, chatting about any and everything. She rides with me to Wal-Mart, Food Depot, the post office, to the bank, every, and anywhere; keeping me company…and I thank God for her!

When she is at home alone at nights, or at home because she lost her job, when she is sad or scared, we keep each other's company and keep the blues away. When people ask, "Aren't you lonely out there in the big house in the woods?" I would answer honestly, "No, I am never lonely." Steiger and I play games, solve puzzles, attend college, and recently started learning Spanish together.

I am awakened each morning by the chirping of blue jays and robins and the ringing of the telephone. At dusk, I watch deer grazing along the pond or a heron that stands silently watching for an opportunity to snatch a fish for dinner. When I walk along the banks of the little stream that meanders through the woods, and count crawfish and ant hills; resting on the little wooden bridge to listen to the rippling of the water and feel the gentle caress of the southern breeze upon my face, I think of Steiger and her wonderful family. I think of Weejay, of Christopher and all my brothers and sisters, nieces and nephews who stay in touch and I thank God for them; may He bless them all. I will never be lonely!

About The Author

Sandra Eugenie Berry (Potts) was born in Portland, Jamaica, West Indies, in 1961. She relocated to Kingston, Jamaica, at age twelve and attended Shortwood Practicing Primary School and Wolmers' High School for Girls. Sandra emigrated to the United States of America in 1987 and she worked on Wall Street for over fourteen years.

Today, she resides in Griffin, Georgia living out one of her lifelong dreams as a registered nurse, caring for the sick.

She is now married to Wendell Johnson, an entertainer, and they have a son, Christopher. Since childhood, Sandy has had a passion for writing short stories and poetry and she aspires to become a playwright.